on London

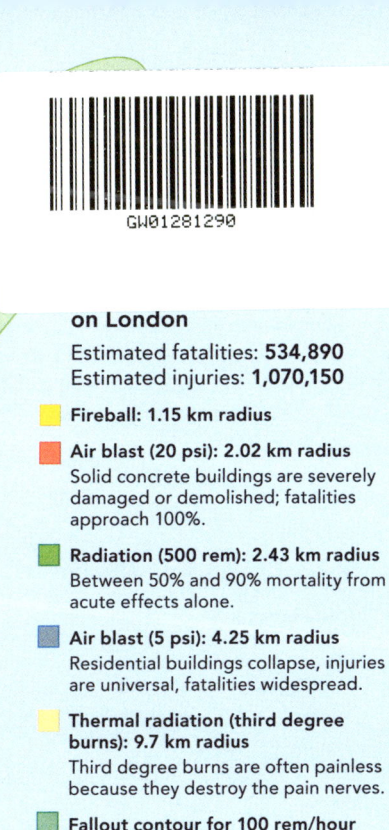

Estimated fatalities: **534,890**
Estimated injuries: **1,070,150**

- **Fireball: 1.15 km radius**

- **Air blast (20 psi): 2.02 km radius**
  Solid concrete buildings are severely damaged or demolished; fatalities approach 100%.

- **Radiation (500 rem): 2.43 km radius**
  Between 50% and 90% mortality from acute effects alone.

- **Air blast (5 psi): 4.25 km radius**
  Residential buildings collapse, injuries are universal, fatalities widespread.

- **Thermal radiation (third degree burns): 9.7 km radius**
  Third degree burns are often painless because they destroy the pain nerves.

- **Fallout contour for 100 rem/hour**
  Approximate area affected: 3,690 km²

- **Fallout contour for 10 rem/hour**
  Approximate area affected: 11,280 km²

Source: nuclearsecrecy.com/nukemap

Series 117

This is a Ladybird Expert book, one of a series of titles for an adult readership. Written by some of the leading lights and outstanding communicators in their fields and published by one of the most trusted and well-loved names in books, the Ladybird Expert series provides clear, accessible and authoritative introductions, informed by expert opinion, to key subjects drawn from science, history and culture.

The Publisher would like to thank the following for the illustrative references for this book:
page 13 graph: FAS Nuclear Notebook

Every effort has been made to ensure images are correctly attributed; however, if any omission or error has been made please notify the Publisher for correction in future editions.

MICHAEL JOSEPH

UK | USA | Canada | Ireland | Australia
India | New Zealand | South Africa

Michael Joseph is part of the Penguin Random House group of companies whose addresses can be found at global.penguinrandomhouse.com

Penguin
Random House
UK

First published 2018
001

Text copyright © Lawrence Freedman, 2018

All images copyright © Ladybird Books Ltd, 2018

The moral right of the author has been asserted

Printed in Italy by L.E.G.O. S.p.A.

A CIP catalogue record for this book is available from the British Library

ISBN: 978–0–718–18889–4

www.greenpenguin.co.uk

MIX
Paper from responsible sources
FSC® C018179

Penguin Random House is committed to a sustainable future for our business, our readers and our planet. This book is made from Forest Stewardship Council® certified paper.

Nuclear Deterrence

Lawrence Freedman

with illustrations by
Duncan Smith

Ladybird Books Ltd, London

Our word 'deterrence' comes from the Latin *deterre* – 'to frighten from or away'. We deter by threatening another with punishment if they act against our interests. Whether or not they are deterred will depend on how seriously they take our threat. Are they confident that the punishment will be inflicted? How much do they value the act we wish to prevent? Deterrence therefore is an act of persuasion. If the target is unconvinced, then deterrence will fail, and it often does. At the same time, we can deter without making explicit threats. Someone might plan to do us harm but then, knowing something about how we are likely to react, decides not to go ahead.

Deterrence is found in nature. Caligo butterflies have owl-eye markings on their wings to discourage small birds from approaching to snap them up. In human affairs, deterrence is regularly at work, from attempts to control naughty children to efforts to reduce crime. In these cases we are well aware that deterrence may fail – because the threats are communicated poorly or are discounted by the target. According to the Bible, the first deterrent threat was when God warned Adam and Eve that if they ate the fruit of the trees of knowledge and conscience in the Garden of Eden, they would be 'doomed to die'. Yet they still disobeyed.

This book is about a particular form of deterrence, employed to prevent war and drawing upon the unprecedented power of nuclear weapons, in which the consequences of failure are too horrendous to contemplate.

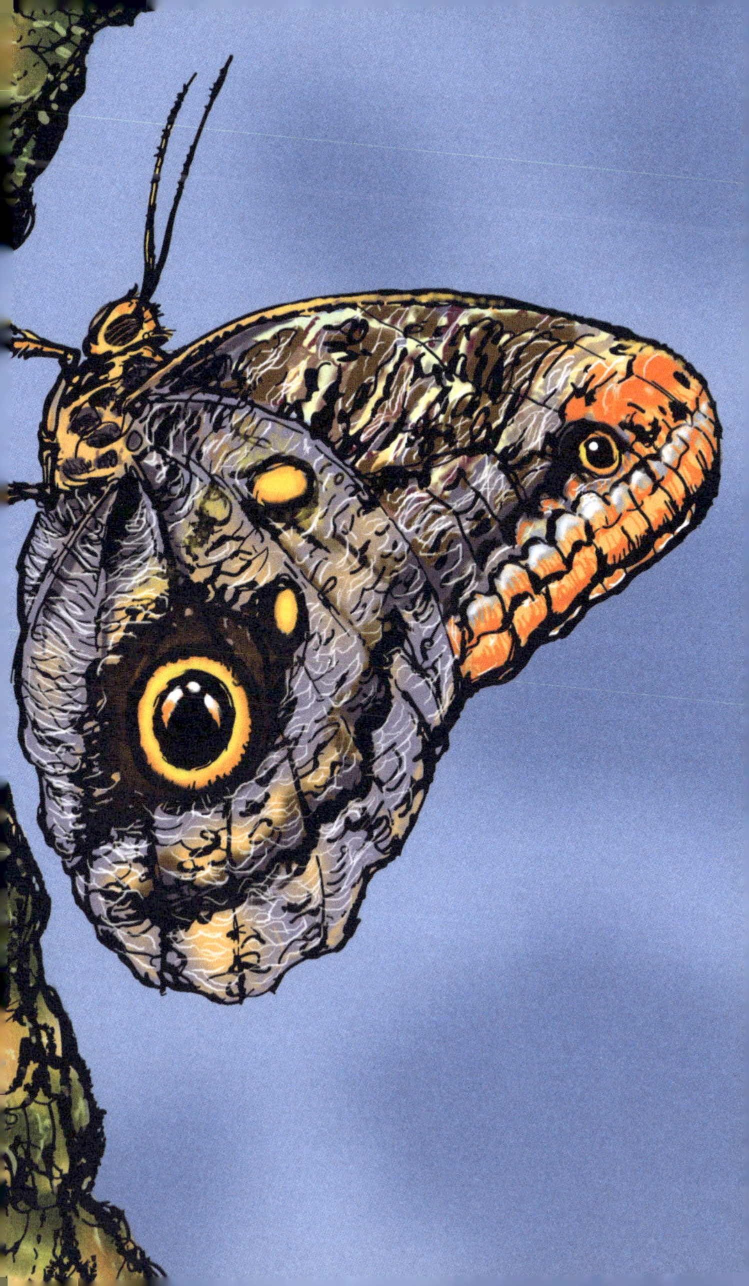

Nuclear weapons resulted from the advances in scientific understanding of the structure of the atom during the first decades of the twentieth century. As the Second World War approached there was a critical breakthrough. A uranium atom could be split into two in a process described as 'fission', releasing a small amount of energy. But if the neutrons released by splitting one atom went on to split others, and these in turn released even more neutrons that went on to split many more atoms, this chain reaction would lead to a massive explosion. For this to happen, a 'critical mass' of fissionable material must be held together. In practice many problems had to be solved before such a bomb could be constructed. But in theory it could be done.

The news stunned the international scientific community. Leo Szilard was one of the first to recognize the possibility of a chain reaction. Fearful that the Nazis would see the potential of a fission bomb, he urged Albert Einstein, the most prestigious scientist of his time, to write to President Roosevelt. The letter reported the possibility of 'extremely powerful bombs of a new type'. Roosevelt took it seriously. In 1942 the Americans established the Manhattan Project, with active British and Canadian participation. This immense scientific and engineering endeavour was tasked to see if fission – or atomic – bombs were feasible, and, if they were, to build them.

Albert Einstein and Leo Szilard

August 2nd, 1939
F.D. Roosevelt,
President of the United States,
White House
Washington, D.C.

In July 1945 the first device was tested in New Mexico. By then Germany had been defeated but Japan had yet to surrender and the US was gearing up to invade the country later in the year. President Truman was looking for a way to bring the war to a quick conclusion and saw the new bomb as one answer.

By this stage of the war terrible destruction of cities had become commonplace. Following the German bombardment of Britain that began in 1940, the US and UK had returned the fire against Germany and Japan, with massive raids causing tens of thousands of casualties in a single night. The atomic bombs dropped on Japan in August 1945 were therefore the culmination of a brutal war, and not even the worst attacks suffered by Japan. In March of that year 100,000 had been killed in the firebombing of Tokyo.

The shock of the atomic bombs lay in their efficiency and the insidious effects of radioactivity. A single bomb (codename 'Little Boy') destroyed the city of Hiroshima on 6 August 1945, killing some 80,000 people immediately. Three days later, a second bomb (codename 'Fat Man') killed some 40,000 in Nagasaki. In both cases the number of fatalities subsequently doubled, with the effects of radiation sickness taking their toll. On 15 August the Emperor of Japan announced his country's surrender, referring to 'a new and most cruel bomb, the power of which to do damage is, indeed, incalculable, taking the toll of many innocent lives'.

'Fat Man' and 'Little Boy'. The two bombs dropped on Japan in August 1945.

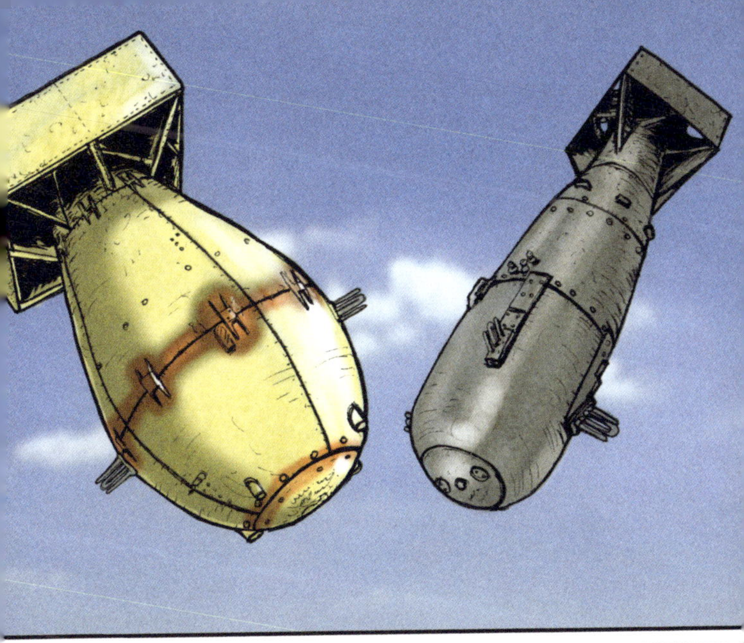
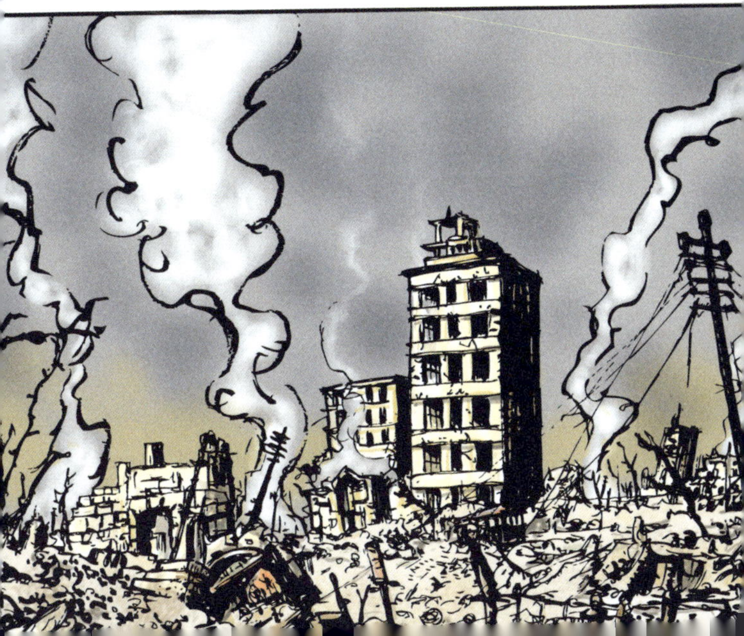

The American monopoly of these weapons did not last long. In August 1949 the Soviet Union tested its own atomic device. In response, the Americans moved to the next stage of nuclear technology, from weapons based on nuclear fission to hydrogen or thermonuclear weapons based on 'fusion'. These weapons promised almost unlimited destructive capacity. In a fusion bomb, the energy from a fission explosion is used to create sufficient energy to squeeze isotopes (deuterium and tritium) of hydrogen together, leading to a massive explosion. The first hydrogen bomb was tested by the US in November 1952. The Soviet Union soon followed.

Whereas atom bombs had explosive yields measured in kilotons (equivalent to thousands of tons of TNT), those of hydrogen bombs were typically measured in megatons (equivalent to millions of tons of TNT). The most powerful bomb ever was one tested by the Soviet Union in October 1961, which reached 57 megatons.

The effects of any bomb in terms of the scale and spread of the damage and casualties would depend on its size and whether it burst on the ground or in the air. Even with the smaller weapons, human beings within a large radius would be killed immediately by blast and fire. Many survivors would be left suffering from severe burns, radiation sickness and psychological trauma. The effects would be felt far away, as radioactive particles (known as 'fallout') would be carried by the wind to distant places, without regard for national boundaries. Over the longer term this would result in a higher incidence of leukaemia and cancer.

> The fusion process releases more energy than the fission process, which is why thermonuclear bombs can be far more powerful than fission ('atomic') bombs.

Nuclear fission

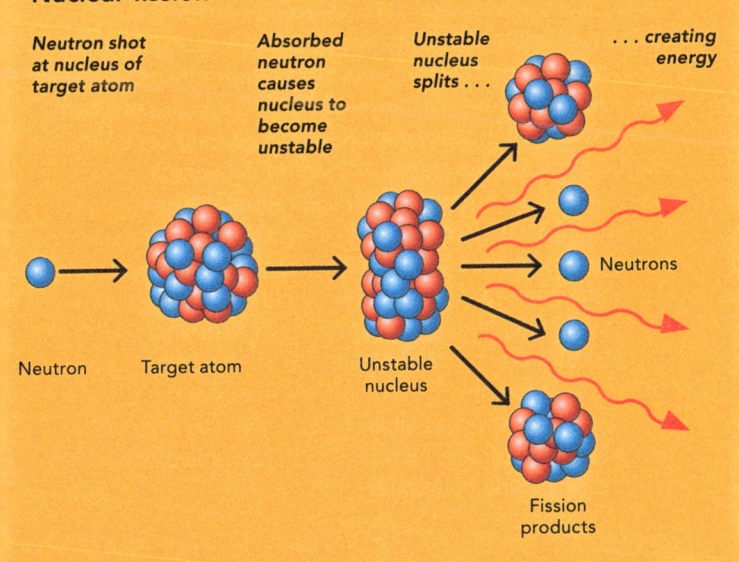

Neutron shot at nucleus of target atom

Absorbed neutron causes nucleus to become unstable

Unstable nucleus splits...

...creating energy

Neutron

Target atom

Unstable nucleus

Neutrons

Fission products

Nuclear fusion

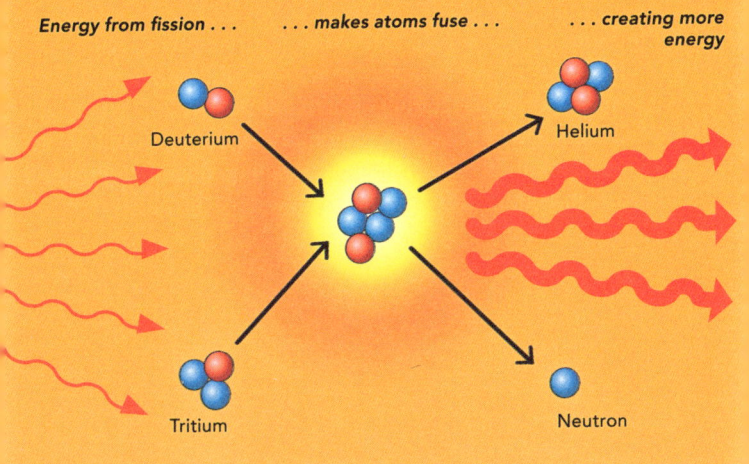

Energy from fission...   *...makes atoms fuse...*   *...creating more energy*

Deuterium

Helium

Tritium

Neutron

Early discussions in the United Nations on preventing the further military exploitation of nuclear energy and concentrating instead on its potential peaceful benefits failed as a result of the intensifying Cold War. Instead, a nuclear arms race developed between the superpowers, the USA and USSR. Each developed a 'triad' of delivery systems: first, long-range bombers; then land-based intercontinental ballistic missiles (ICBMs); and lastly submarine-launched ballistic missiles (SLBMs). Ballistic missiles are launched with sufficient initial power to set them off on a trajectory that will take them to their targets. Later cruise missiles, pilotless aircraft that can be launched from air, sea or land, were added to the mix. Weapons with the range to be used by the two superpowers against each other were described as 'strategic'. 'Tactical' weapons were more likely to be utilized in a battle between regular forces.

The number of weapons grew dramatically. From very few in 1950, by the end of that decade the United States had over 20,000 weapons. The stockpile peaked in 1967 at more than 30,000. The Soviet stockpile was still in the low hundreds in 1960 but then grew rapidly, peaking at some 40,000.

Other powers soon joined in. No longer able to work with the US after the war, Britain decided to build an independent force to preserve its standing as a major power. It tested an atomic bomb in 1952 and a version of a hydrogen bomb in 1957. Cooperation with the Americans then resumed. France tested its first atomic bomb in 1960.

Combined nuclear stockpiles

USA
China, India, Israel & Pakistan
France & UK
Russia

The Cold War began as the Second World War ended. As the Soviet Union extended its grip over Central and Eastern Europe, the United States became committed to the security of Western Europe. Deterrence in the first instance was based on alliance, marked by the formation of the North Atlantic Treaty Organization (NATO) in 1949. Moscow would think twice before taking on the military strength of the United States.

Nuclear weapons were a vital part of this strength, a point emphasized in 1954 when the United States warned that it would respond to any aggression with 'massive retaliation'. Yet nuclear weapons also appeared to be a declining asset. The Soviet Union would catch up and a Third World War would be even more horrific than the previous one. Robert Oppenheimer, the leader of the Manhattan Project, described the superpowers as being like 'two scorpions in a bottle, each capable of killing the other, but only at the risk of his own life'. The fallout generated by regular nuclear tests showed how vulnerable all humanity had become.

Soon a paradox was noted. This terrifying prospect provided strong incentives to be cautious at times of crisis. In March 1955, in one of his last speeches as Prime Minister, Winston Churchill commented on the 'sublime irony' that a stage had been reached 'where safety will be the sturdy child of terror, and survival the twin brother of annihilation'. War was becoming too dangerous to be used as an instrument of policy.

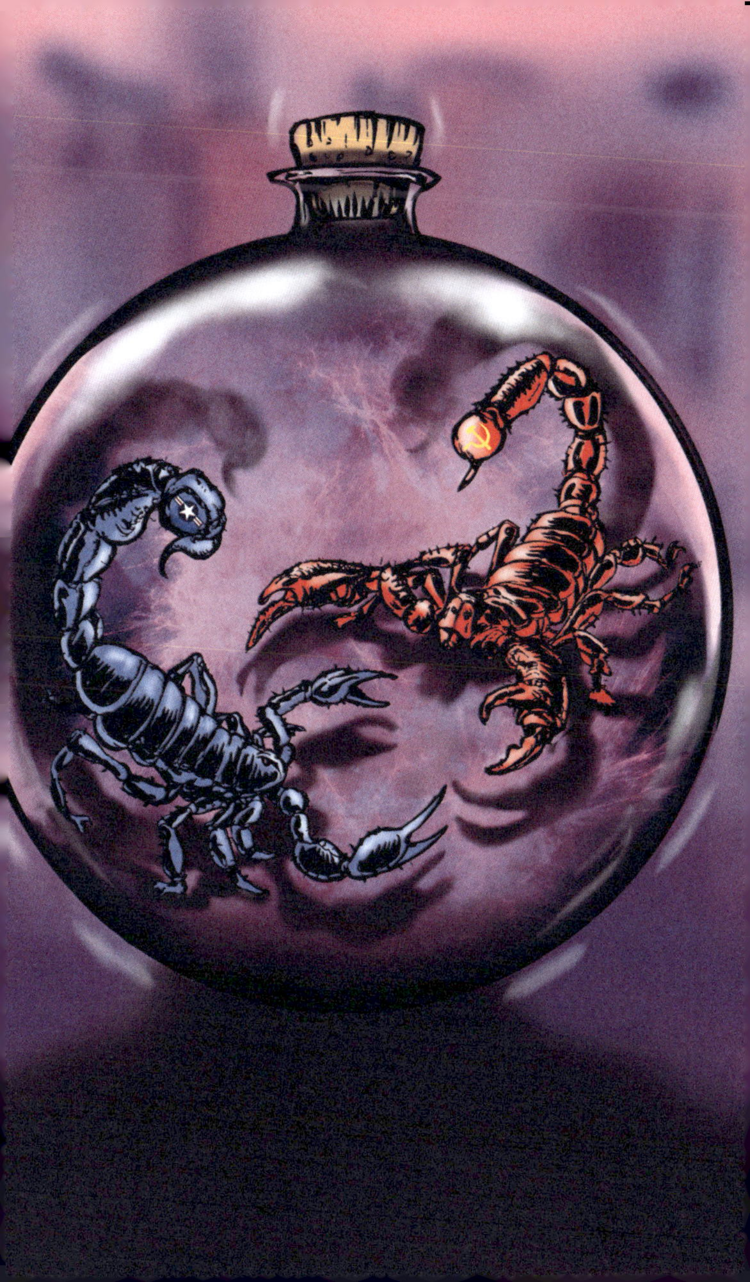

Was this 'balance of terror' stable? Civilian strategists explored the possibility of a nuclear 'first strike' disarming the opponent. This would require developing a force that could catch the enemy in a surprise attack, taking out the opposition's bombers in their bases, missiles in their underground silos and even submarines at sea. Any missiles that escaped the attack and did get launched would need to be destroyed before they reached their targets. Disarmed and unable to retaliate, the victim would be at the attacker's mercy. Victory could be declared. A 'second-strike' capability described the ability to avoid such an outcome by absorbing a first strike and still being sure of mounting an effective riposte.

If one side had a first-strike capability, the other would be anxious until it was able to reduce its vulnerabilities. If both sides had a first-strike capability, then the situation could become very unstable, as both would be on edge, fearful that they might be caught with a knockout blow.

Imagine a classic Western showdown. The sheriff and the outlaw move towards each other, hands close to guns, ready to draw. Everything depends on firing first and with accuracy. Hesitation or a miss means death. But what if instead of guns they have poisoned darts? There is now no premium on firing first. The victim will still have enough time to retaliate before the poison takes effect. In such circumstances it would be sensible to be cautious, and maybe try diplomacy.

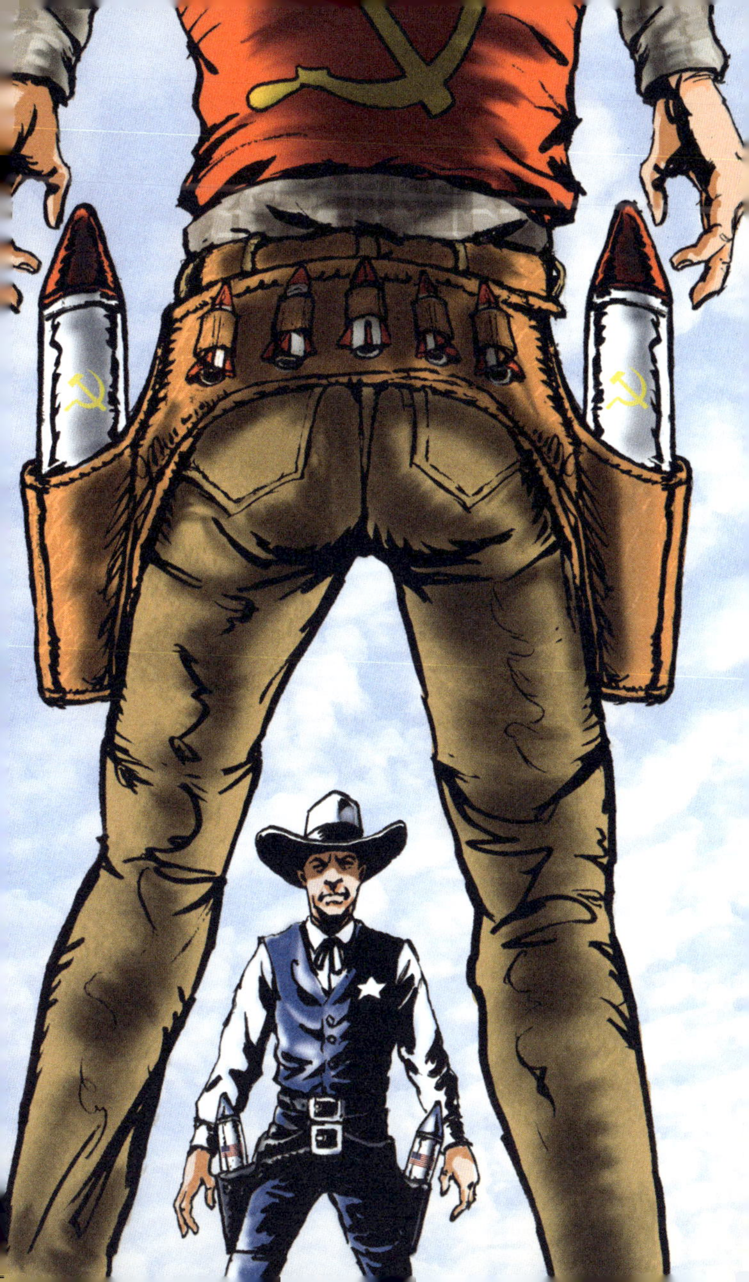

The requirements of a successful first strike would be demanding:

- complete surprise, though at a time of intense crisis the enemy would be on guard;
- confidence in systems that had never been tested before in such a complex operation;
- excellent intelligence about the targets that must be hit, with none missed out;
- sufficient weapons to cover all targets and the lethality and accuracy to ensure all are destroyed;
- meticulous planning to attack disparate targets at approximately the same time.

The amount of warning received by the enemy would be a critical factor. With enough warning, the enemy might be able to launch a second strike before the first strike reached its targets, so that only empty bases and missile silos would be destroyed.

A 'launch on warning' strategy could be reckless. It would depend on early-warning systems that were known to be fallible. Once a flock of geese picked up on radars was interpreted as incoming missiles. To avoid getting caught by surprise, the RAF used to keep aircraft at the end of runways, on 'quick reaction alert', ready to take off at the first news of enemy attack.

The main reason why the idea of a first strike became progressively less plausible was the placement of missiles on submarines. Submarines powered by their own nuclear reactors, staying quiet and rarely surfacing, were difficult to find, track and attack. Despite regular talk of breakthroughs in anti-submarine warfare, SLBMs remained by far the least vulnerable part of the nuclear arsenal.

Quick reaction alert. An RAF crew race to their waiting Vulcan bomber.

Ring!

If a retaliatory attack was launched, might incoming aircraft or missiles be shot down in flight? During the Second World War anti-aircraft guns took a heavy toll on bombers but still some always got through. Against nuclear weapons the performance standard of defences has to be so much higher. If any missiles get through, the consequences will be catastrophic. Yet ballistic-missile defences face a far greater challenge than air defences: far less warning of an incoming attack and its probable targets. All big cities and vital areas would need to be protected, as the enemy could choose where to attack. If the radar system were knocked out, the defences would be blinded. If chaff and spoofs were added, the defences could be fooled. If more warheads were added, the defences could be overwhelmed. This became even more likely once multiple independently targeted re-entry vehicles (MIRVs) could be put on top of each missile. UK Trident submarines carry up to eight missiles and forty warheads (but they could carry more).

Once warheads broke through and began exploding, even less could be done, especially for those close to 'ground zero', the point of the explosion. The only possible protection would be against fallout. Fallout shelters made the most sense when built well away from likely explosions. When governments distributed advice on how to survive a nuclear attack, the impact was often to add to the readers' sense of hopelessness. And, given the likely post-attack conditions, one question was whether the survivors would envy the dead.

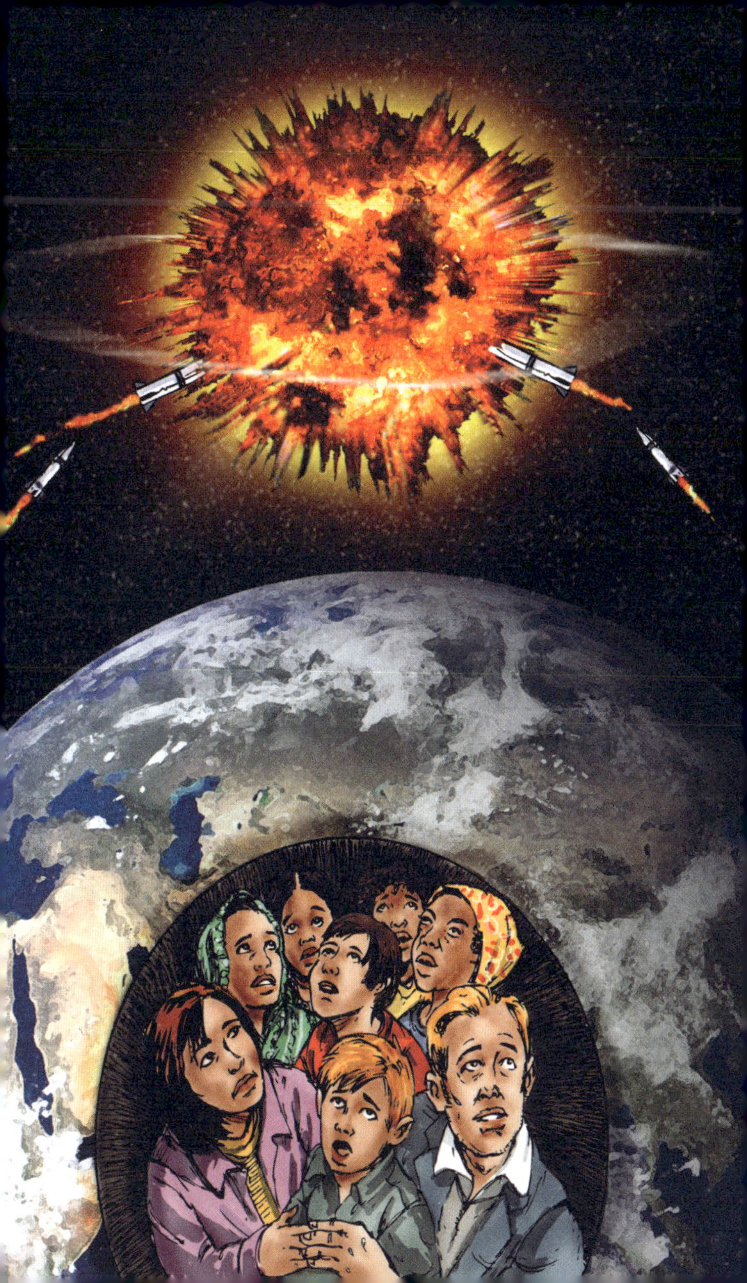

For all these reasons, by the mid 1960s the US government had concluded that even though it still enjoyed superiority in number of weapons the situation was one of 'mutual assured destruction', known as MAD. The level of required destruction set for the Soviet Union in the Pentagon was up to 30 per cent of its industrial capacity and two-thirds of its population. That was set not as a target so much as a demonstration of a second-strike capability. In practice after this point extra weapons landing on Soviet territory would make little difference, only making the 'rubble bounce'. MAD meant the US faced the same sort of devastation.

This prospect encouraged political leaders not to let any crisis get out of hand. One flashpoint was Berlin, a city divided between East and West and located in East Germany. In 1961 communist leaders were alarmed that the city was being used by people escaping to the West. Soviet leader Nikita Khrushchev appeared determined to force Western powers out of Berlin, but instead a wall was built to keep people in. The next year a more dangerous crisis resulted when the US discovered that the Soviet Union was building bases for its short-range nuclear missiles in communist Cuba, close to the US mainland. President John F. Kennedy demanded the withdrawal of the missiles and began to blockade Cuba. After some tense days, when neither side seemed ready to back down, Khrushchev agreed to withdraw in return for a promise that the US would not invade Cuba.

Kennedy and Khrushchev. The Cuban missile crisis, October 1962.

CONFIDENTIAL
630 NM
350 NM
HAVANA
Havana
Guanajay
IRBM Site
San Diego
de los Banos
Bay of Pigs
Guantanamo Bay
HONDURAS
HONDURAS
SECRET
CANAL
ZONE

Both crises demonstrated that neither side wanted the Cold War to turn into a Hot War. MAD suggested that the two vast nuclear arsenals now effectively neutralized each other. This is how nuclear deterrence is often still understood: one nuclear capability deters another's potential use. But did that mean that war could continue with the sort of armed forces used in previous wars – so-called conventional forces – without turning into a nuclear war? Would a side that was losing accept defeat rather than risk moving to this hugely destructive form of warfare?

This was a serious issue for NATO because the Warsaw Pact, the Soviet Union's alliance, was assumed to be stronger in conventional forces while enjoying a geographic advantage. All Soviet forces could be put into battle from the start, while American reserves would need to get across the Atlantic, at risk from Soviet submarines. By the time full US support reached Europe the war might be lost. For this reason, NATO always insisted that it would be prepared to 'go nuclear' if losing the conventional battle.

This was a much more ambitious form of nuclear deterrence, known as 'extended deterrence'. It required the US to meet its alliance obligations by threatening to use nuclear weapons in response to conventional aggression even though its own territory was not then under attack. Yet in order to protect Berlin, Paris, Brussels or London it would be putting New York, Washington and Chicago at nuclear risk. Could such a threat be credible?

East versus West: the Cold War alliances.

EUROPEAN ALLIANCES DURING THE COLD WAR

NATO (formed 1949)

- Belgium
- Canada
- Denmark
- France
- Iceland
- Italy
- Luxembourg
- Netherlands
- Norway
- Portugal
- United Kingdom
- United States
- Greece (1952)
- Turkey (1952)
- Germany (1955)
- Spain (1982)

Neutral and non-aligned
- Austria
- Finland
- Ireland
- Malta (after 1979)
- Sweden
- Switzerland
- Yugoslavia

Warsaw Pact (formed 1955)

- Albania (until 1968)
- Bulgaria
- Czechoslovakia
- East Germany
- Hungary
- Poland
- Romania
- USSR

Deterrence might work best if nuclear threats were implemented automatically, but no US president would take a step that could be tantamount to national suicide without careful thought. Such careful thought would make it less likely that the threat would be implemented. Accordingly, from the early 1960s the Americans sought to persuade NATO countries to build up their conventional forces to reduce dependence on nuclear threats. The European view was that deterrence was working fine. The smallest risk of nuclear war was enough to ensure Soviet restraint, while easing that risk meant that another ferocious conventional war became more likely. That might spare the American and Soviet homelands but would still devastate the centre of Europe. Building up conventional forces would also be expensive. Eventually, in 1967, NATO agreed to adopt the strategy of 'flexible response', preparing to deal with aggression by conventional means if possible but nuclear means if necessary.

Out of this debate came an important distinction. If deterrence was about persuading an opponent that the prospective gains from a particular act would be outweighed by the prospective costs, then the opponent's calculations could be influenced by demonstrating that it would be hard to make gains as well as that costs would be severe. 'Deterrence by denial' came to refer to preventing gains; 'deterrence by punishment' to imposing costs. Nuclear weapons focused attention on punishment but denial would be preferable, because the enemy would know that there would be no point in even trying to make gains.

A display of military might during Moscow's annual Victory Day parade.

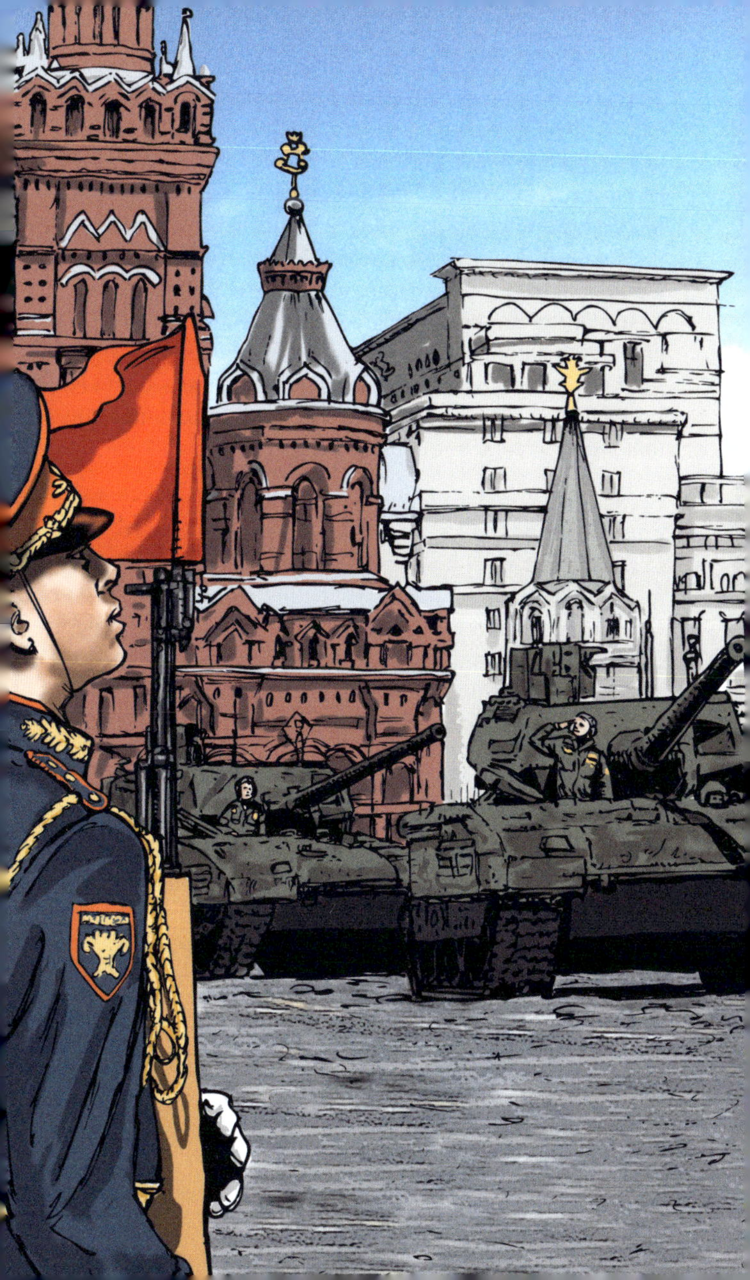

Another way to reduce the risk of a strategic nuclear war was to develop a class of tactical nuclear weapons (TNWs) that could boost conventional forces. These weapons would be powerful versions of standard munitions, from mines to depth charges to artillery shells. The difficulty was that even the smallest, low-yield nuclear weapons of a few kilotons would still have a devastating impact, and if used in numbers would demolish the area which was being fought over. The concept of escalation was developed to explain why it was unlikely that any war involving nuclear weapons could be limited. A step on to the moving staircase would take you to a higher level without the possibility of going back.

Escalation could be a way of reinforcing deterrence. A war might begin at a conventional level but then pass a threshold to the nuclear level because of battlefield considerations, and then move inevitably on to the higher strategic level. Others argued that the concept was overdone. One strategist, Herman Kahn, for example, described an 'escalation ladder' with forty-four rungs, which included almost thirty ways of using nuclear weapons, from demonstrations to reinforce an ultimatum, to striking military targets (counter-force), to tentative attacks against cities (counter-value), to all-out war. His point was that the development of a war could be controlled. The more mainstream view was that after the first fateful steps one type of nuclear use would merge into another.

During the 1950s the US Army tested low-yield weapons in battlefield conditions.

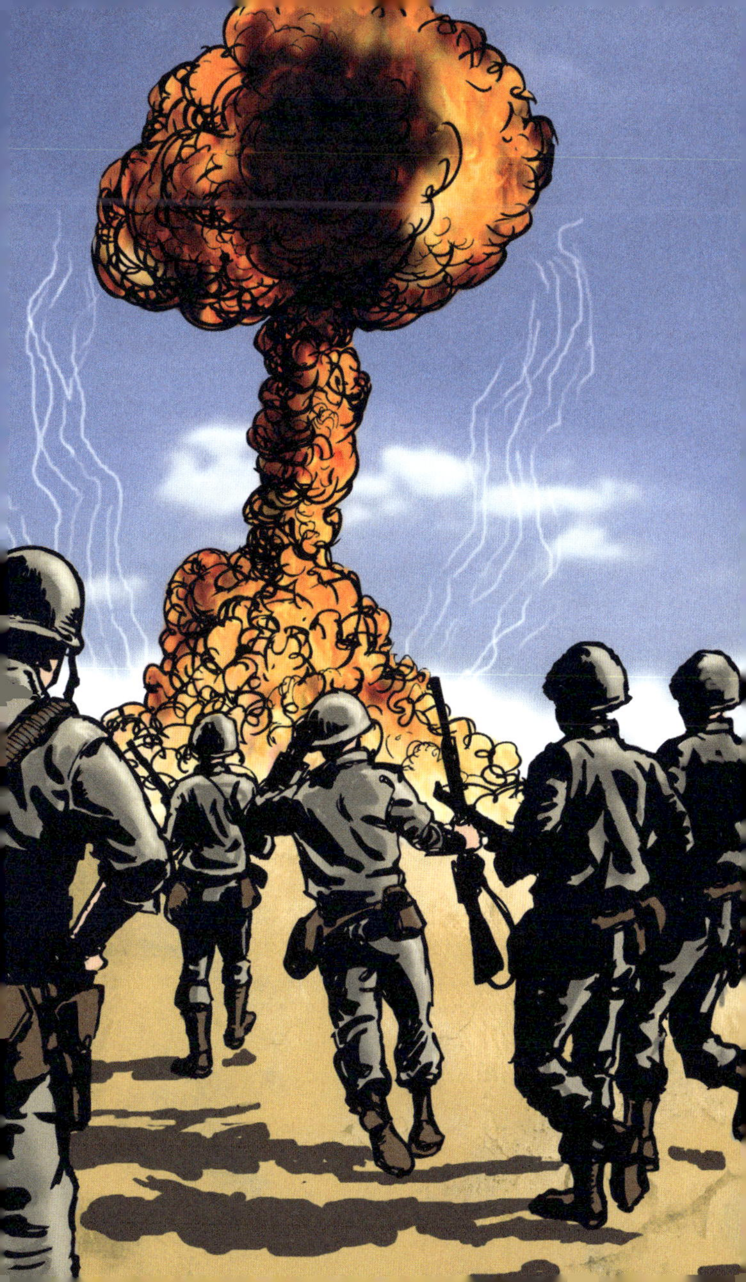

The themes of push-button destruction and mass death were soon picked up in popular culture. Little credence was given to the idea that deterrence would hold indefinitely. Civil defence preparations were regularly satirized for their futility and nuclear strategists mocked for their jargon and insensitivity to the implications of their apparently technical studies.

TV programmes took nuclear conflict as their subject. *The War Game* (not shown by the BBC because it was considered too upsetting) explored in a documentary style the brutal aftermath of a nuclear war on ordinary communities, with food shortages, traumatized children and looters being shot. Films, including *Fail Safe* and *Dr. Strangelove*, pointed out how a terrible war might occur because of accidents or recklessness. They explored types of weapons that were never actually developed, such as a 'doomsday machine' that would send a devastating riposte automatically once enemy strikes were detected, or 'cobalt bombs' designed to prolong the effects of fallout so that whole areas would be uninhabitable for years. Nevil Shute's 1957 novel *On the Beach* had humanity's only survivors waiting in Australia for the fallout resulting from numerous cobalt bombs to reach them. When anxiety about nuclear war became prevalent again in the early 1980s, these themes reappeared, for example in the drama-documentary *The Day After*, which described the breakdown of social norms as individuals struggled to survive, or Raymond Briggs's comic book *When the Wind Blows*, which highlighted the bleak position of individuals once the missiles had been launched, as they tried to follow the advice of a civil defence pamphlet.

In 1964 Stanley Kubrick's *Dr. Strangelove (Or How I Stopped Worrying and Learned to Love the Bomb)* satirized deterrence theories.

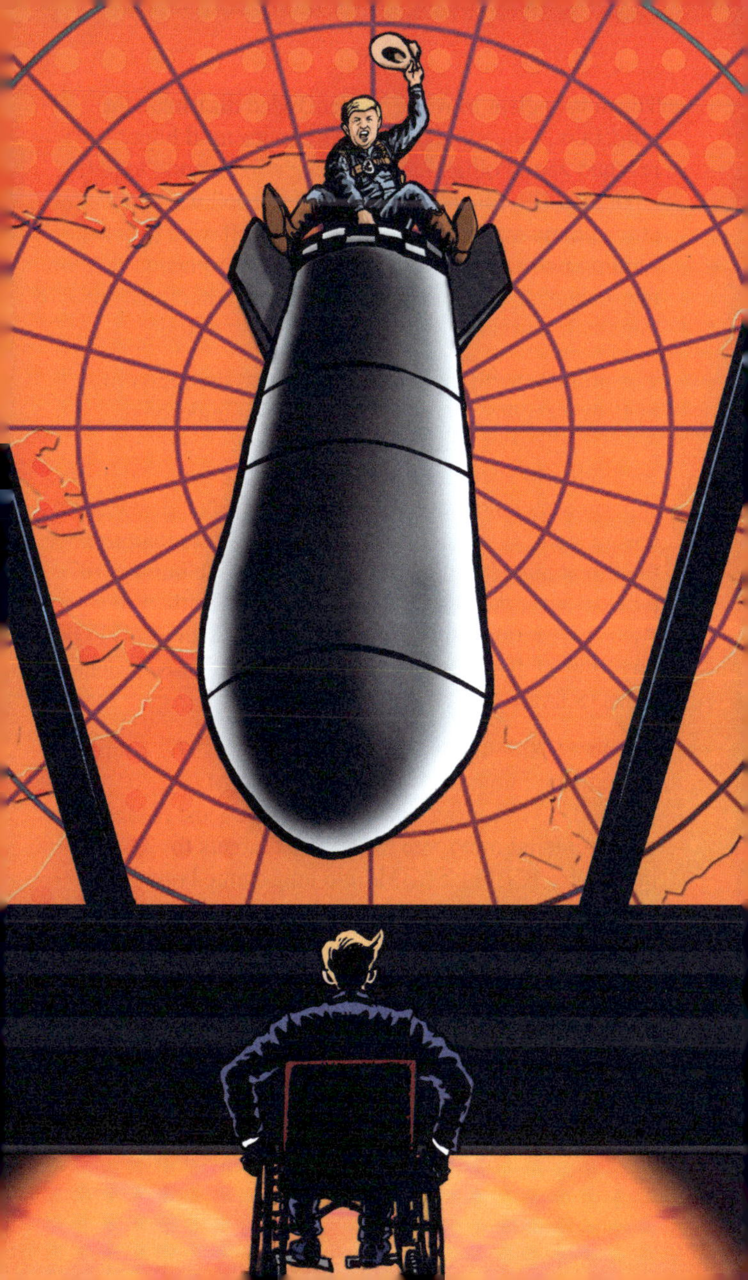

The anti-nuclear movements demanded disarmament, reduction in the numbers of all weapons until hopefully they reached zero. Political leaders sought to respond to public anxieties. The first measure agreed in 1963 was to prohibit atmospheric nuclear testing. This was followed by bans on sending nuclear weapons to outer space or placing them on the seabed. A 'hotline' was introduced so that the leaders of the major powers could talk to each other at times of crisis.

The problem with disarmament was that the secret of nuclear weapons was now known, and if underlying political disputes were not resolved, states would not trust each other to stick to agreements. Instead, from 1969 the superpowers embarked on arms-control talks, designed to ensure stability in nuclear relationships rather than remove the threat altogether. This meant capping the number of types of weapons. These were known first as the Strategic Arms Limitation Talks (SALT) and then, with a nod in the direction of disarmament, as the Strategic Arms Reduction Talks (START).

The first SALT agreement, signed in May 1972, confirmed the existing numbers of ICBMs and SLBMs – 1,710 for the US, and 2,348 for the Soviet Union. The most recent treaty, which entered into force in 2011, set targets for 2018 of 800 in total for ICBMs, SLBMs and long-range bombers, of which up to 700 could be deployed and with a sub-limit of 1,550 for the nuclear armaments installed on these deployed systems. So the overall numbers are well down since the late 1960s. The inventories, however, are still huge.

The Campaign for Nuclear Disarmament's first march to the Atomic Weapons Establishment at Aldermaston in 1958.

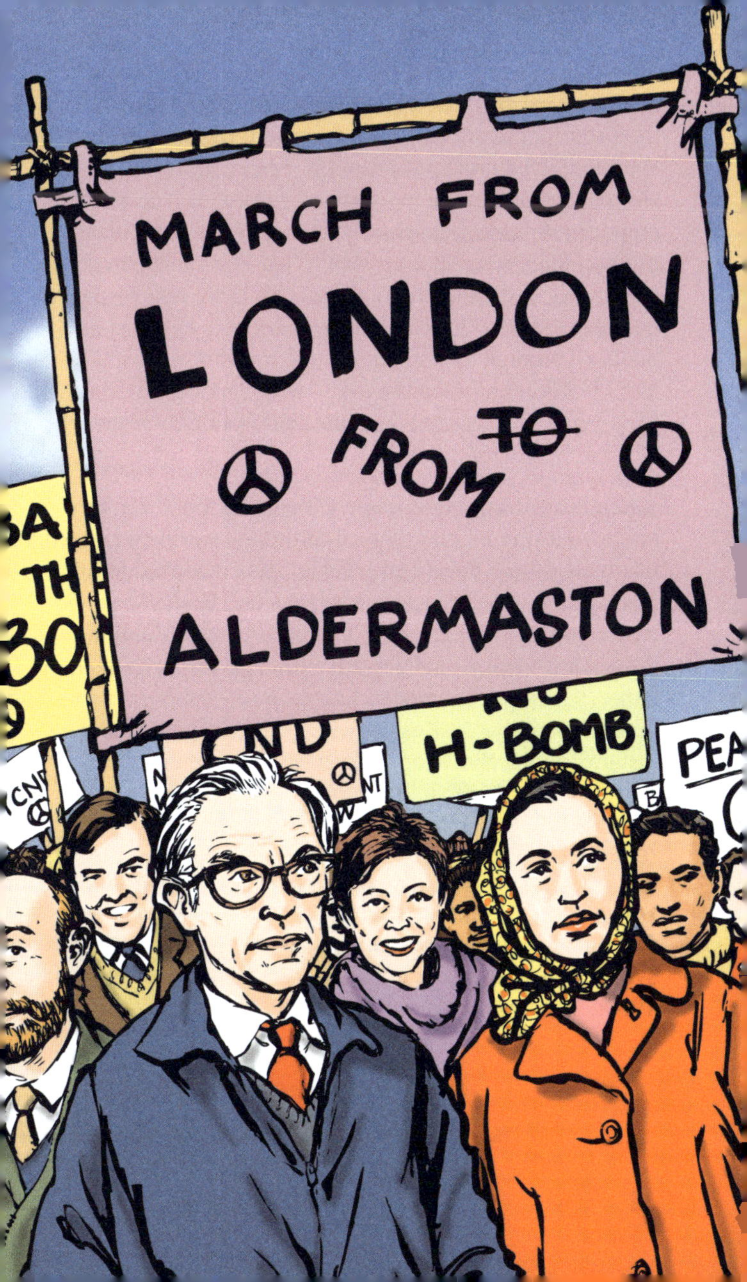
MARCH FROM
LONDON
~~TO~~ FROM
ALDERMASTON
H-BOMB

A continuing arms race between two superpowers, plans for a war that could end civilization and regular nuclear tests generated great public alarm. For many, it was simply immoral to attempt to achieve national security by preparing for mass slaughter. Others pointed to the dangers of miscalculation and accidents. What would happen if the control systems malfunctioned? Or there was a rogue nuclear commander? Or a crazy leader, like Hitler in his bunker, prepared to bring the whole world down with him? Thinking of numerous ways to use nuclear weapons appeared madness when just one could cause a catastrophe beyond imagination.

When President Reagan came to power in 1981, the anti-nuclear movement was revived across the world by concerns that he was both deeply anti-Soviet and convinced in the belief that a nuclear victory was possible. His 1983 proposal to develop a comprehensive defensive system (dubbed 'Star Wars') that would prevent Soviet missiles reaching American targets seemed to fit a desire to achieve a first-strike capability. Yet Reagan had nurtured a long-standing distaste for nuclear weapons, hence his preference for 'protecting' rather than 'avenging'. His Star Wars scheme exceeded the technological possibilities and was never constructed. His anti-communism made it hard for him to do deals with Moscow. But when a reformer, Mikhail Gorbachev, came to power, Reagan saw an opportunity. In 1985 the two men agreed that a 'nuclear war can never be won and must never be fought'.

In 1987 Presidents Ronald Reagan and Mikhail Gorbachev signed a treaty eliminating their countries intermediate nuclear forces.

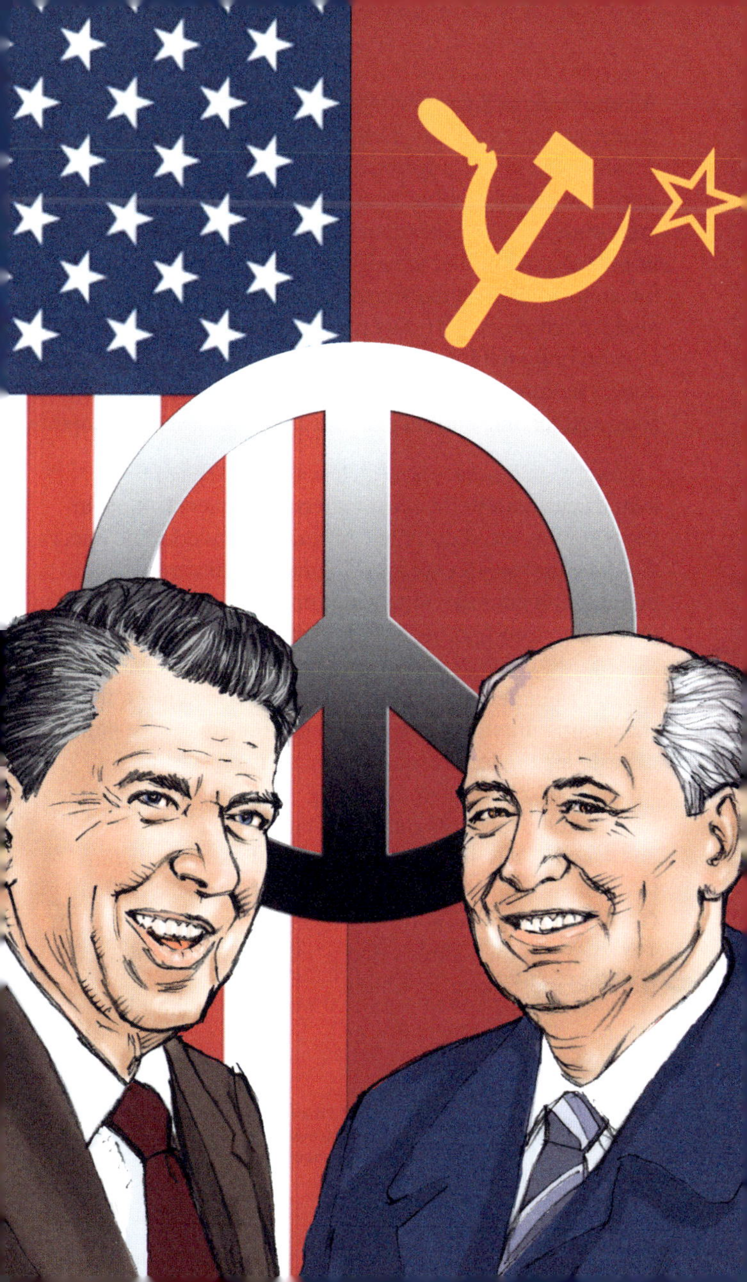

When the Cold War effectively ended with a breach in the Berlin Wall in November 1989 this peaceful conclusion was attributed to nuclear deterrence. It was not the only factor. The prospect of another non-nuclear war was a compelling argument for restraint. Also the superpowers had learned how to manage crises to stop them getting out of hand. Yet it was evident from the comments and memoirs of political leaders that the prospect of nuclear war weighed heavily. A 'crystal ball effect' was at work. It was hard to be confident about the success of aggression when it was possible to foresee a terrible end result.

This supposed success of nuclear deterrence led to a disturbing thought. If it had enhanced the security of the superpowers and their allies, perhaps it could do the same for other states with their own security concerns. After Britain, France and China tested weapons, it was expected that many others would follow. A number of candidates were identified – India, Sweden, Japan, Taiwan, Brazil, Argentina, India, Pakistan, Israel and Egypt. The superpowers viewed this prospect with alarm. Additional nuclear states would complicate crises and create dangerous instabilities.

A Non-Proliferation Treaty (NPT) came into force in 1970. It was a remarkably unequal treaty – described as drunks requiring abstinence from others. All states other than the five established nuclear powers were prohibited from acquiring nuclear weapons. In return, the nuclear powers were to negotiate in 'good faith' measures leading to 'general and complete' (not just nuclear) disarmament.

> The 'crystal ball effect' meant that political and military leaders could be in no doubt about the risks they would be running in a Third World War.

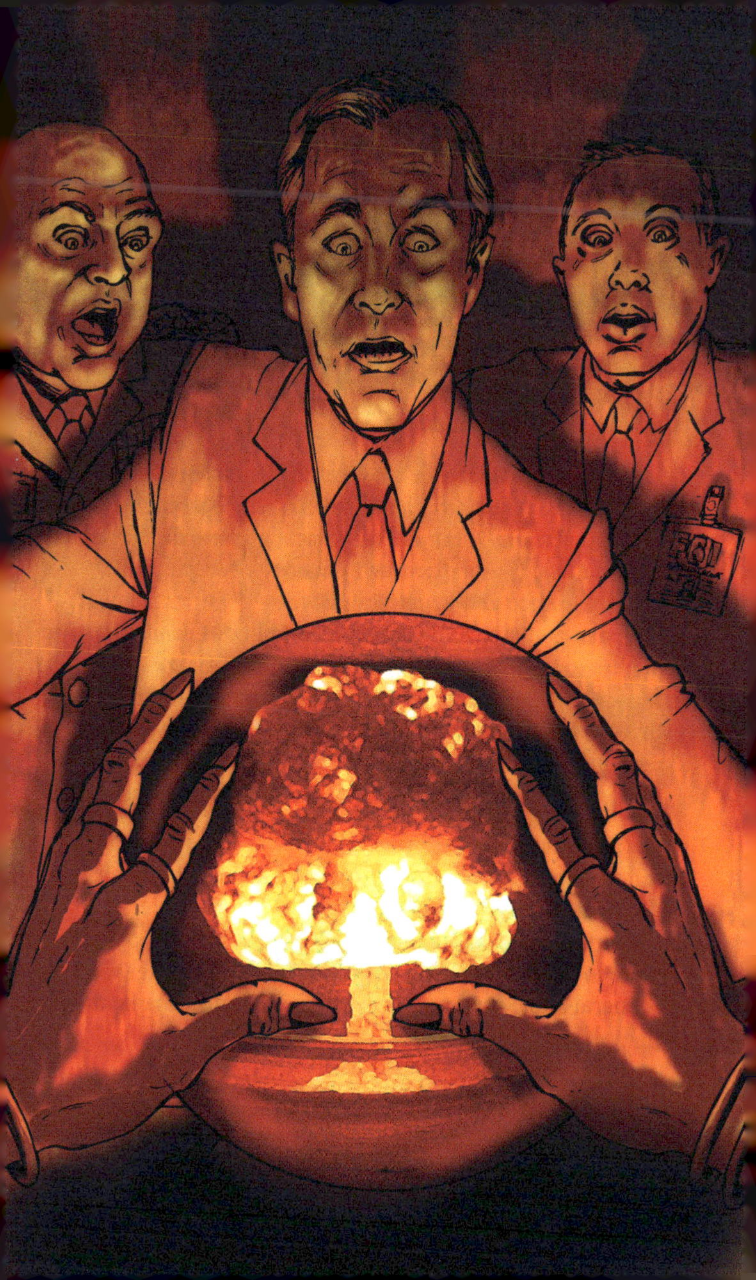

Treaties also have a deterrent effect. There is a stigma to breaking them. Most countries that ratified the NPT kept to its terms. In addition, states contemplating the acquisition of nuclear weapons faced substantial practical obstacles. Nor could they expect to keep a nuclear programme secret. At first the prestige attached to demonstrating the technical and engineering know-how was a motive but over time that appeared less important. Those countries in alliance with the United States preferred to rely on extended deterrence as a more credible alternative to trying to construct their own independent deterrents.

Some countries had a real nuclear capability and changed their minds. South Africa constructed six weapons, but, with the end of white minority rule seeming imminent, it decided to dismantle the weapons and joined the NPT in 1991. Ukraine inherited about a third of the old Soviet nuclear arsenal when it became independent in 1991, although it did not have operational command, which remained with Moscow. Kazakhstan and Belarus were in a similar position. In 1994 Ukraine agreed to return the weapons to Russia in return for security guarantees. These guarantees did them little good when Russia invaded in 2014, leading many Ukrainians to wonder whether they would have been better advised to hold on to the missiles as a deterrent.

A number of countries stayed outside the NPT (Israel, India and Pakistan) or else ratified the treaty but ignored its restraints (Iraq, Iran and North Korea). In all these cases the basic motivation was security. They wanted their own nuclear deterrents.

Nuclear weapons stockpiles, 2018

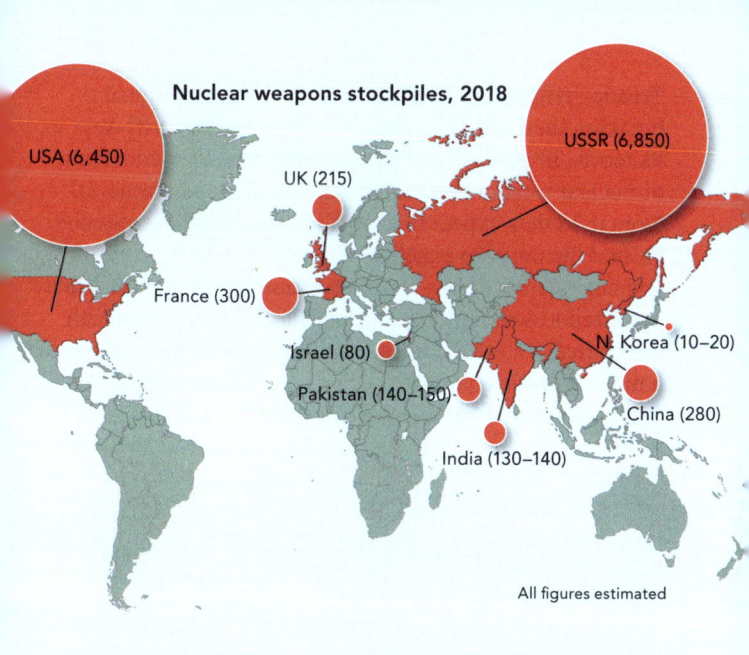

- USA (6,450)
- USSR (6,850)
- UK (215)
- France (300)
- Israel (80)
- Pakistan (140–150)
- India (130–140)
- China (280)
- N. Korea (10–20)

All figures estimated

Countries that once had nuclear options

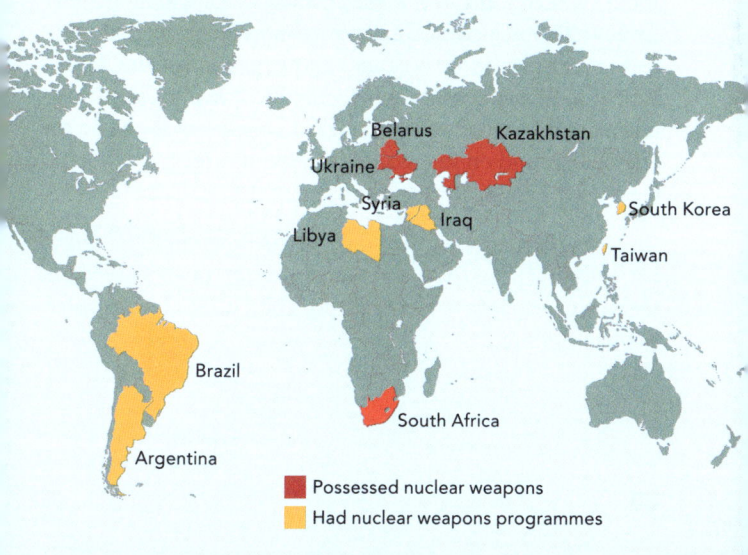

- Belarus
- Kazakhstan
- Ukraine
- Syria
- Iraq
- Libya
- South Korea
- Taiwan
- Brazil
- Argentina
- South Africa

■ Possessed nuclear weapons
■ Had nuclear weapons programmes

Britain described its nuclear force as a contribution to NATO's deterrent. To explain why this was needed when there was also the US nuclear guarantee, the official line was that this would provide a 'second centre of decision'. Even if Moscow doubted that Washington would hesitate before retaliating to aggression, it would also have to consider the possibility that London would be more robust. In addition, an independent force was a hedge against a changing US role. Because Britain bought its missiles (but not the warheads) from the US, and serviced them at a joint facility, its actual independence has been questioned. Its four missile-carrying submarines are, however, under national command. France's *force de frappe* reflected even more an assertion of independence and reluctance to rely on the US. Its missiles were to be directed *tous azimuts*, against threats from all directions. Both countries stress the importance of having at least one submarine on patrol all the time.

China's original nuclear programme also reflected doubts about its major ally, the Soviet Union, despite their shared communism. China tested an atom bomb in 1964 and a hydrogen bomb in 1967. Two years later the Soviet Union appeared to contemplate a pre-emptive strike before China had an operational capability. It held back, but the scare led China to gear its first missiles, during the 1970s, to deterring the Soviet Union. Now they are more geared to the United States, as China builds up its conventional strength and asserts its regional interests.

A Royal Navy submarine test launches a Trident missile.

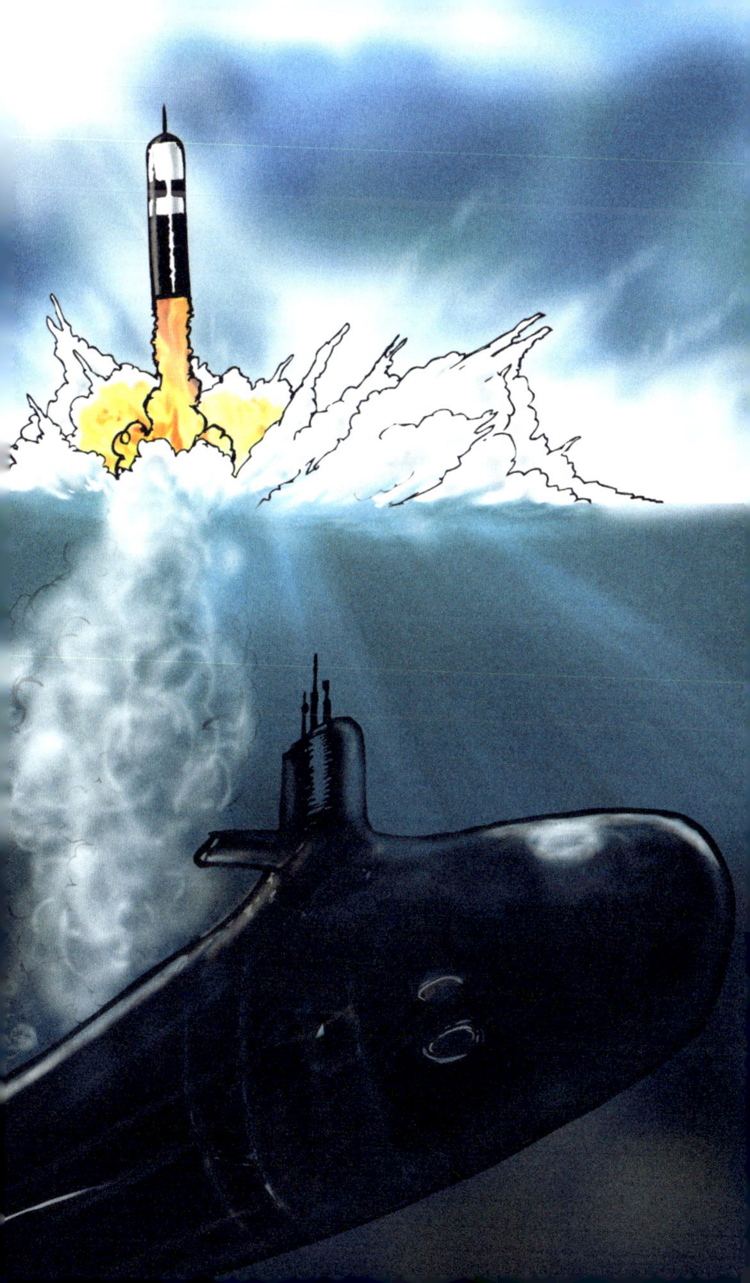

India and Pakistan have fought a number of wars since 1947, leaving a legacy of mistrust as well as unresolved differences. India acquired nuclear weapons because of China and to keep the upper hand over Pakistan. One Pakistani leader observed that the country must 'eat grass' rather than fall behind. In 1998 the two countries tested weapons one after the other. Both now have substantial arsenals. This became a major test of deterrence. Could skirmishes and even limited war take place without escalating to nuclear use? If major war looked likely, would India be tempted to try a first strike against Pakistan? What about the security of Pakistan's weapons in the event of major internal instability? The government insisted that they were safe from seizure by extremist groups.

A key figure in the Pakistani project, A. Q. Khan, sold nuclear know-how to a number of other would-be proliferators, including North Korea, a militarized and isolated country. Negotiations to close down North Korea's nuclear programme began in 1994 but despite occasional agreements it pressed on, with its first test in 2006. In 2017 the issue came to a head with the new American president, Donald Trump, threatening 'fire and fury' as the North began testing an ICBM that could hit the US. The next year tensions eased as North Korean president Kim Jong-un met with Trump, with great fanfare. This showed how even a small nuclear arsenal could raise a country's international standing. There was a promise to 'denuclearize' the Korean Peninsula but no agreement about what this meant in practice or a timetable.

North Korean leader Kim Jong-un is briefed on his country's nuclear programme.

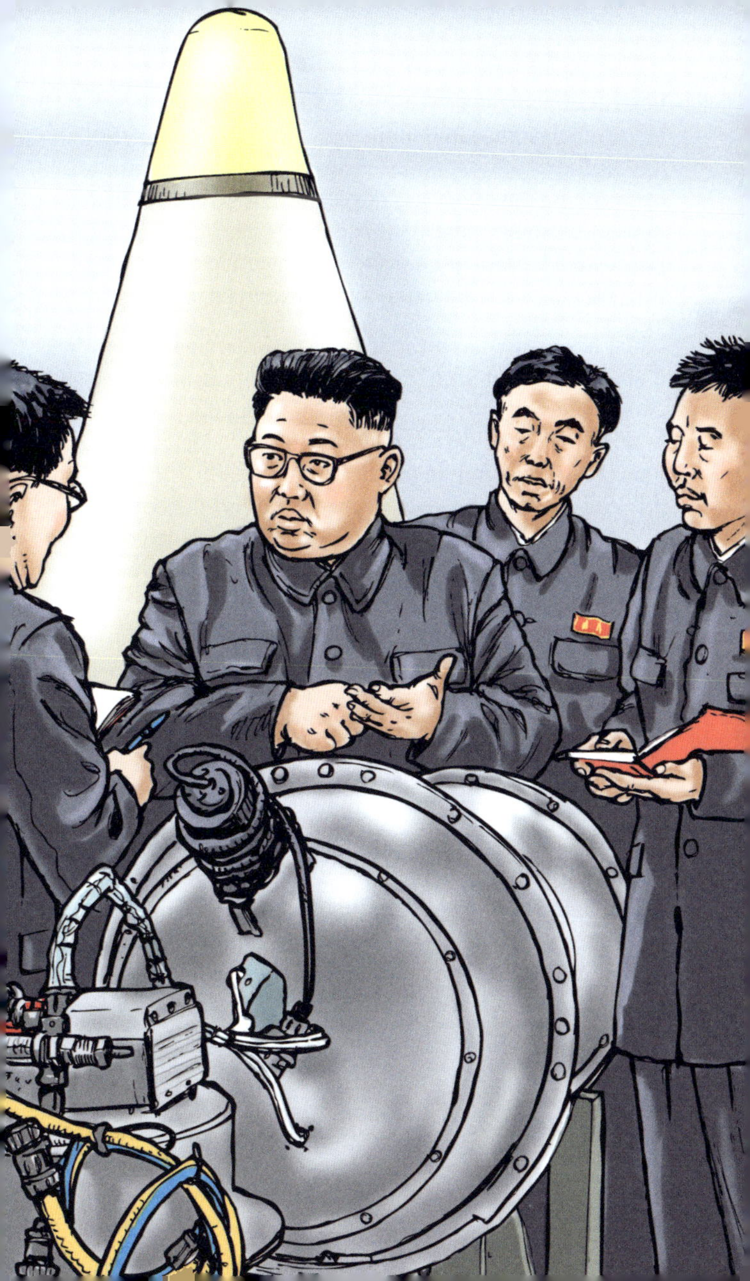

Fearful of being overwhelmed by its neighbours, Israel began nuclear research in the 1950s, with French help, to develop a weapon of last resort. Its success became an open secret, but Israel has never formally admitted that its nuclear weapons exist. This capability has helped deter Arab governments from attempts to eliminate Israel in a major war, but has not deterred lesser wars and terrorism.

Israel has worked to prevent other regional powers building their own nuclear weapons. It destroyed reactors under construction in Iraq in 1981 and Syria in 2007. Iraq's leader, Saddam Hussein, was determined to have a deterrent against Israel as well as Iran (against which it fought a long war in the 1980s). It might have succeeded but for the occupation of Kuwait in 1990 which led to war with a US-led coalition. The ceasefire agreement required that its nuclear facilities be dismantled. (Allegations that Iraq was violating its terms led to the 2003 US-UK invasion of Iraq.)

Iran had long felt that its regional status should be matched by a nuclear status. Its efforts to enrich uranium to weapons-grade quality were discovered in 2002. Despite international sanctions, it resisted demands to abandon these efforts. In 2015 it agreed to redesign, convert and reduce its nuclear facilities in return for sanctions being lifted. In May 2018 President Trump said that the US no longer accepted the agreement and re-imposed sanctions. Concern that Iran will revive its programme is one reason for other countries, such as Saudi Arabia and Egypt, to consider starting their own.

Israeli F-16s hit Iraq's Osirak nuclear reactor in June 1981. The Israelis claimed that the reactor, bought from France in 1976, was about to go critical.

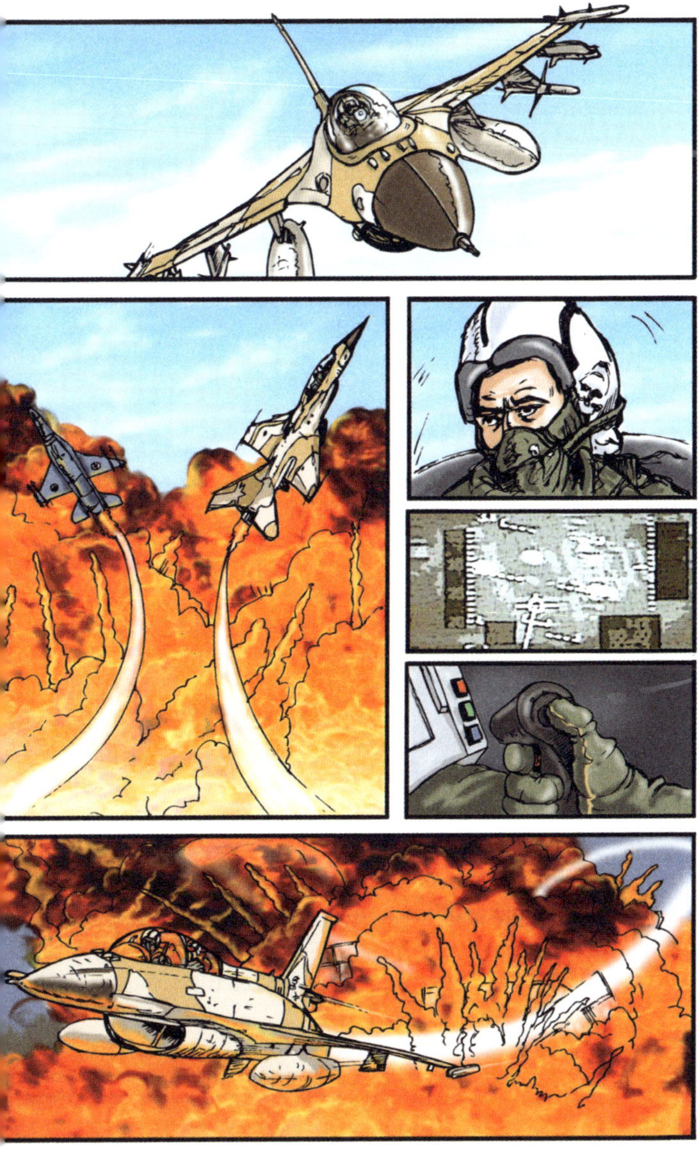

The attacks on the United States of 11 September 2001, when mass casualties were caused by terrorists hijacking commercial airliners and turning them into lethal weapons, generated anxiety that groups such al Qaeda might try to get hold of true weapons of mass destruction (WMD) – chemical and biological as well as nuclear weapons. One concern, and part of the rationale for the 2003 invasion of Iraq, was that a state such as Iraq might pass WMD on to terrorist groups as a means of getting at its major adversaries. There was no evidence for this.

Another concern, widely expressed after the collapse of the Soviet Union, was that extremist or criminal groups might acquire 'loose nukes' – poorly guarded weapons that were vulnerable to theft.

The most challenging option for terrorists would be to build their own weapons. The basic science is well known and designs could be found on the internet, but it would be necessary to get hold of fissionable material and skilled scientists and engineers, and then keep this dangerous, difficult work secret.

A less demanding challenge would be to build 'radiation weapons', which would require the sort of radioactive materials that can be found in research labs or hospitals. Their effects would be limited, largely rendering an area uninhabitable.

Terrorists could cause mayhem relying on guns, knives and traditional explosives without WMD. But if they did get hold of such weapons, deterrence would be of little relevance as they would quickly be used.

If terrorists got hold of nuclear materials, the dangers could come in many forms.

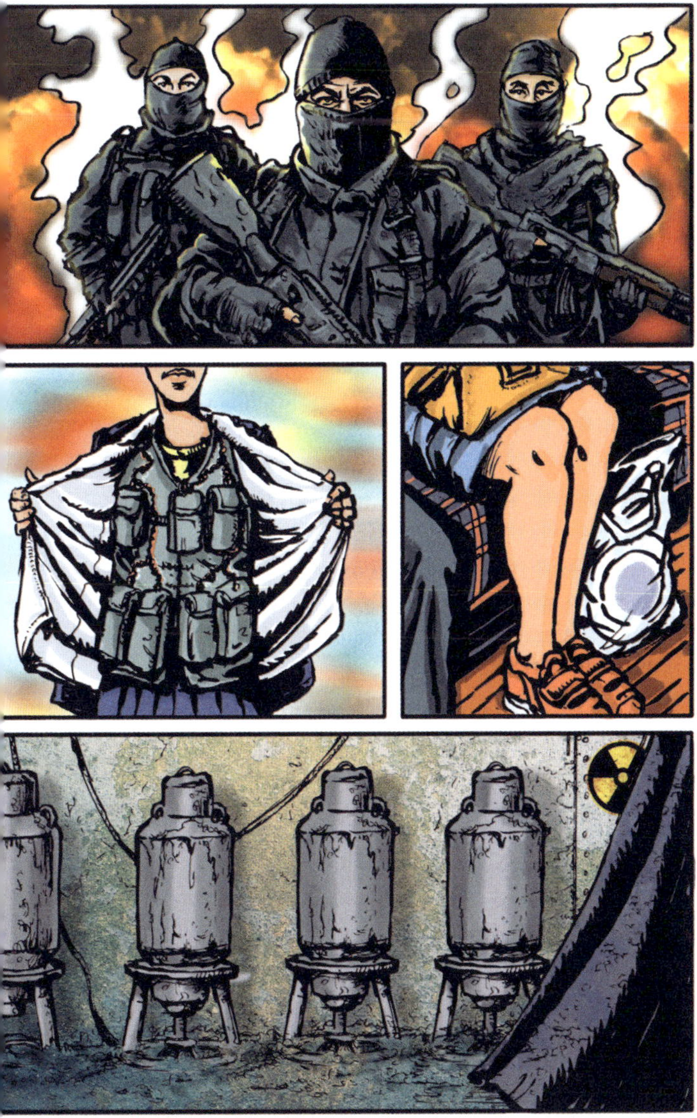

The concepts behind nuclear deterrence, and the weapons supporting them, were products of the Cold War. When that was over, it was widely assumed that nuclear deterrence would become less prominent in security policies – with fewer systems, more stress on safety, and slow rather than fast reactions. In the event there was more continuity than change. In the US there was seen to be no need to move away from the triad of bombers, ICBMs and SLBMs, and all are being modernized. President Obama declared himself in favour of a nuclear-free world in April 2009 but the American posture would not alter so long as Russia sustained its own active nuclear capability. After President Putin seized Crimea in 2014, he reminded the West that Russia was a nuclear superpower, just in case there were any thoughts of intervening on behalf of Ukraine. Then continuing conflict over Ukraine led NATO members that had been part of the old Soviet Union, such as Estonia, to feel threatened. The question of US extended deterrence came to the fore again. President Trump's review of nuclear policy led to proposals to build up the US arsenal and develop more 'usable' weapons.

One potential source of challenge to assumptions about assured destruction was new technologies. Might it be possible to disable command systems by cyberattacks and so prevent missiles being launched, or send them off in the wrong direction? Will a report of a breakthrough in anti-submarine warfare one day turn out to be true? Might credible defences against long-range missiles emerge out of the technologies currently being applied to deal with short-range missiles?

One question for the future is the vulnerability of nuclear command systems to cyberattacks.

It is hard to identify any rational strategy for nuclear use that would not carry a risk of terrible retaliation or else already be pointless because deterrence had failed and the homeland had suffered massive destruction. This is why the deterrent effect of nuclear weapons lies not in specific threats or scenarios but in the compelling thought that once a war begins there is no telling where it will stop. At issue is not the certainty that devastating weapons will be used but just the possibility that they might.

This thought has helped prevent another world war or any use of nuclear weapons since August 1945. Though there is no shortage of conflict, the very worst has been avoided. It would be remarkable if this continued and the record were still in place as the end of this century approaches. One detonation, or just a few, would not necessarily mean the end of deterrence. The shock might serve as an awful reminder of the dangers of war, encouraging restraint and more strenuous efforts at disarmament. But it could also ease existing inhibitions and lead to a greater catastrophe.

Action can be taken to reduce stockpiles but dismantling weapons and disposing of fissile material is complicated and time-consuming. The most urgent tasks therefore remain political: working on alternatives to deterrence by marginalizing nuclear weapons in security policies, stigmatizing all attacks on populations, addressing the sources of conflict, improving mechanisms for dispute resolution, keeping forms of communication open at all times, and encouraging positive forms of cooperation.

The Doomsday Clock was first displayed by the Bulletin of Atomic Scientists in 1947. It is currently set at two minutes to midnight.

Further reading

This book draws on two previous works of mine, which readers may find helpful if they wish to explore the issues raised further: Lawrence Freedman, *Deterrence*, (Polity Press, 2004) and Lawrence Freedman, *The Evolution of Nuclear Strategy*, (Palgrave, 2004). This is the third edition. A fourth edition is forthcoming.